Contents

About the Book

"Nothing succeeds like success."
—Alexandre Dumas the Elder, 1854

And no other math resource helps kids succeed like *Scholastic Success With Math!* For classroom or at-home use, this exciting series for kids in grades 1 through 6 provides invaluable reinforcement and practice for math skills such as:

❑ number sense and concepts
❑ reasoning and logic
❑ basic operations and computations
❑ story problems and equations
❑ time, money, and measurement
❑ fractions, decimals, and percentages
❑ geometry and basic shapes
❑ graphs, charts, tables … and more!

Each 64-page book contains loads of challenging puzzles, inviting games, and clever practice pages to keep kids delighted and excited as they strengthen their basic math skills.

What makes *Scholastic Success With Math* so solid?

Each practice page in the series reinforces a specific, age-appropriate skill as outlined in one or more of the following standardized tests:

◎ *Iowa Tests of Basic Skills*
◎ *California Tests of Basic Skills*
◎ *California Achievement Test*
◎ *Metropolitan Achievement Test*
◎ *Stanford Achievement Test*

These are the skills that help kids succeed in daily math work and on standardized achievement tests. And the handy Instant Skills Index at the back of every book helps you succeed in zeroing in on the skills your kids need most!

Take the lead and help kids succeed with *Scholastic Success With Math.*
Parents and teachers agree: No one helps kids succeed like Scholastic!

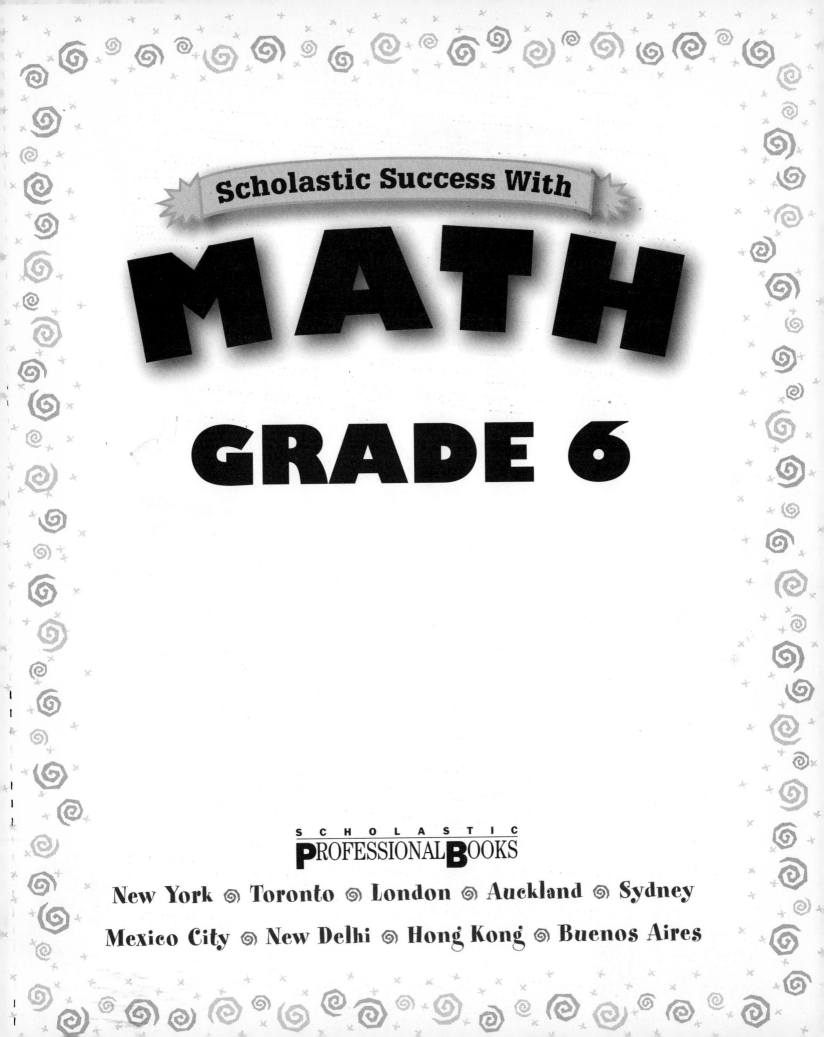

Scholastic Success With

MATH

GRADE 6

SCHOLASTIC
PROFESSIONAL BOOKS

New York ◎ Toronto ◎ London ◎ Auckland ◎ Sydney

Mexico City ◎ New Delhi ◎ Hong Kong ◎ Buenos Aires

Compiled and produced by Susan L. Lingo, Bright Ideas Books™

Cover design by Maria Lilja

Cover art by Victoria Raymond

Interior design by Ellen Matlach Hassell
for Boultinghouse & Boultinghouse, Inc.

ISBN 0-439-41970-0

Math Whiz

Name _____   Date _____

Figure It Out!

1. Itchy Squirrel scores 86, 73, 47, 93, and 81 on her math tests. What is her high score? What is her low score?

_____

2. The range of Itchy's scores is the difference between her high and low scores. What is her range? _____

3. Arrange Itchy's scores in problem 1 from lowest to highest. The median is the middle score in the group. What is her median score? _____

4. The mean score is the average score. To find the mean, add all the scores. Then divide the total by the number of scores. What is the mean of Itchy's scores in problem 1?

_____

5. The mode is the score that appears the most in a group. Find the mode from this group of quiz scores: 16, 15, 18, 20, 15, 13, 15, 13, 19. _____

SUPER CHALLENGE: Roll a number cube 25 times. Record the scores. Find the range, mean, median, and mode of your scores.

5

Amazing Primes

Name _____ Date _____

Find your way through the maze from start to finish without crossing over any composite numbers. You must pass over all 15 prime numbers between 1 and 50 at least once.

Estimating Sums & Differences

Name _____ Date _____

 1 When two whole numbers are each rounded to the nearest ten, the sum is 80. One of the addends is the greatest number that rounds to 30. The second addend is the least number it can be.

What is the sum of the two numbers? _____

 2 The sum of two whole numbers, each rounded to the nearest hundred, is 7,000. One addend rounds to 3,400. The other addend is the largest whole number it can be.

What number is it? _____

 3 Rounded to the nearest hundred, the sum of two numbers is 11,000. Each addend is the greatest number it can be. One addend has 4 digits and the other has 3 digits.

What are the numbers? _____

 4 If two numbers are each rounded to the nearest thousand, their sum is 50,000 and their difference is 10,000. Each is the greatest number it can be, given those conditions.

What are the numbers? _____

Prime Ice Cream Bandits

Name _____ Date _____

✏ Irving's Ice Cream Factory is filled with tasty flavors. There's Plum Raisin Supreme, Apple Banana Swirl, Broccoli Chocolate Chunk, and many more. But Irving has a big problem. Some of his workers have been secretly eating pints of their favorite flavors. But who are the culprits? Prime numbers have the answer.

Directions:
◆ Look at the numbers on the workers' shirts.
◆ Circle the T-shirts that have prime numbers on them. (Hint: Try dividing the numbers by those you've already identified as prime.)
◆ Those workers are the ice cream bandits!

Work with a friend to make a list of ten more prime numbers.

Whirling Triangles

Name _____ Date _____

If the number has a 3 in the thousandths place, color the shape green.
If the number has a 3 in the hundredths place, color the shape yellow.
If the number has a 3 in the tenths place, color the shape blue.
Finish the design by coloring the
other shapes with the colors
of your choice.

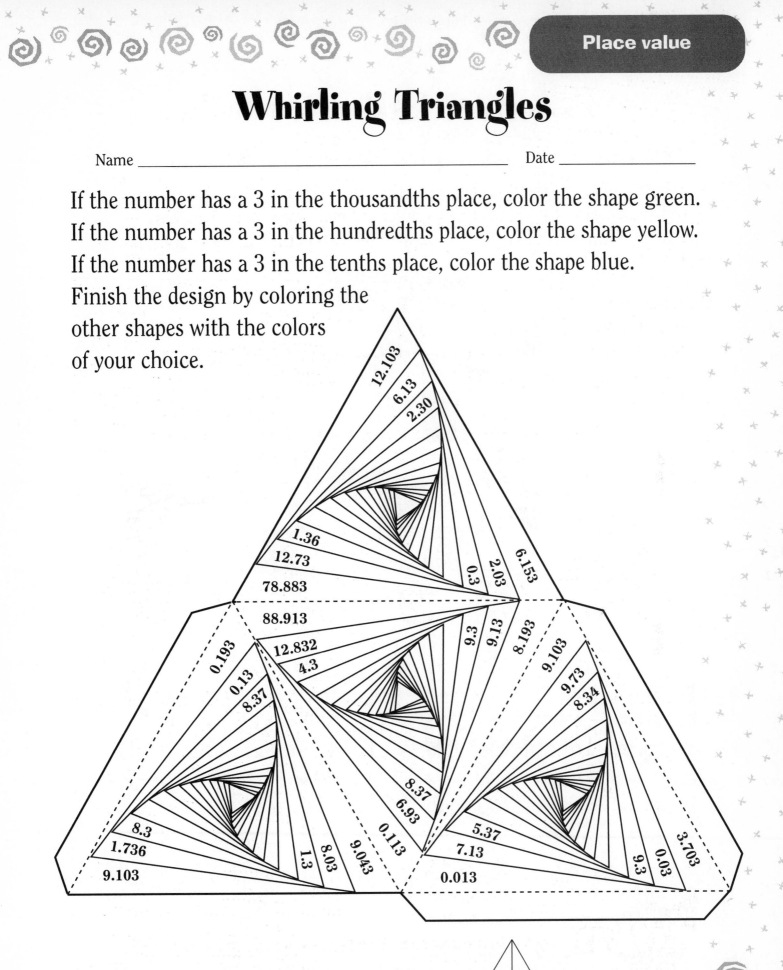

For more fun, cut out the design and fold it into a △.

Best Estimator

Name _____ Date _____

Use estimation to solve these problems. Circle the most likely answer.
Then write the answer in the crossnumber puzzle.

ACROSS:

A.	16.98 + 18.99	36	26
C.	24.85 + 29.99	65	55
E.	21.99 + 8.95	31	41
G.	218.04 + 67.90	286	386
I.	53.75 + 40.98	105	95
K.	7.99 + 19.70	28	22
L.	99.98 + 99.57	300	200
M.	65.75 + 20.90	87	97
O.	9.69 + 32.99	40	43
P.	588.95 + 14.90	704	604
Q.	3.75 + 9.99	13	14
R.	428.70 + 50.90	480	520

DOWN:

B.	28.59 + 33.95	69	63
C.	39.25 + 18.70	58	42
D.	376.35 + 184.50	521	561
F.	7.28 + 11.69	19	16
H.	199.80 + 224.99	525	425
J.	399.95 + 126.99	527	566
M.	5.85 + 76.95	83	75
N.	39.80 + 13.99	54	62
O.	26.98 + 16.89	44	49
P.	48.95 + 18.99	68	66

I wish I could do it!

All Mixed Up

Name _____ Date _____

Finding the sums is easy. But when you try to put
these numbers correctly in the puzzle, you'll find
yourself all mixed up!

Find the sum and write the answer in the puzzle. Each digit can occupy only one place
to make the whole puzzle fit together perfectly. The first one has been done for you.

54 + 98 **152**	69 + 37	31 + 85	292 + 614	589 + 92	261 + 97
423 + 79	180 + 98	349 + 301	2,012 + 2,106	413 + 923	855 + 723
1,617 + 1,281	4,068 + 784	1,602 + 639	5,142 + 2,690	1,069 + 1,103	1,597 + 346
4,115 + 106	1,022 + 1,886	951 + 1,384	12,401 + 6,001	44,595 + 13,816	5,354 + 1,346

Pattern Block Maze

Name _____ Date _____

If you can find your way through the pattern block maze from start to finish without crossing over any shapes with numbers that are divisible by 2, 3, or 4, you are a superstar. If you
find a path where none of the numbers are divisible by 2, 3, or 4 and the sum of the numbers equals 389, you are a genius! A path may be formed by connecting a corner or a side.

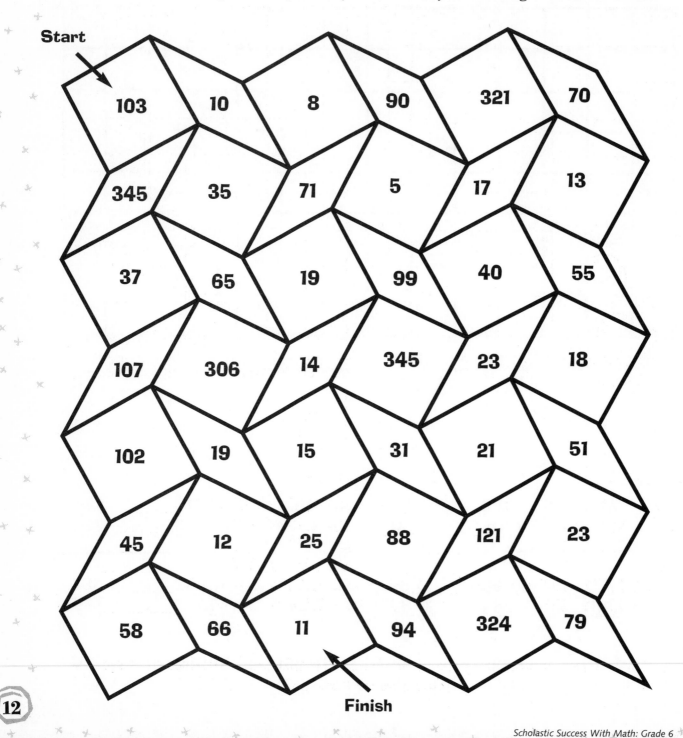

Fun Times

Name _____ Date _____

Do the multiplication problems at the bottom of the
page, and place the answers in the crossword puzzle.

Across

A.	24	x	16 = _____
B.	410	x	103 = _____
D.	392	x	145 = _____
F.	997	x	817 = _____
H.	1,157	x	102 = _____
J.	1,168	x	455 = _____

Down

A.	375	x	86 = _____
B.	418	x	119 = _____
C.	342	x	102 = _____
E.	1,056	x	467 = _____
G.	1,122	x	507 = _____
I.	1,194	x	365 = _____

By the way, do you know why the person who made this puzzle got fired from her job?

¡spɹoʍ ssoɹɔ ʎuɐɯ ooꓕ

Adding & Multiplying

Name _____ Date _____

 1 Two counting numbers are three apart. Their sum is 47.

What are the numbers? _____

 2 The product of two consecutive numbers is 210.

What are the numbers? _____

 3 The sum of two twin primes is 60.

What are the numbers? _____

 4 Three consecutive numbers have a sum of 135.

What are the numbers? _____

5 The product of three consecutive odd numbers is 6,783.

What are the numbers? _____

6 Two numbers have a product of 676 and a quotient of 4.

What are the numbers? _____

Crisscross Number Puzzles

Name _____ Date _____

Solve the subtraction problems. Each of the eight 4-digit answers fits into the puzzle below. One digit must be placed in each box to form a 4-digit number in each row (from left to right) and each column (from top to bottom). The clues will help you decide where to place the numbers.

1) $\begin{array}{r} 30{,}771 \\ -\ 29{,}419 \end{array}$ 2) $\begin{array}{r} 16{,}570 \\ -\ 13{,}292 \end{array}$ 3) $\begin{array}{r} 70{,}610 \\ -\ 62{,}410 \end{array}$ 4) $\begin{array}{r} 49{,}905 \\ -\ 47{,}559 \end{array}$

5) $\begin{array}{r} 11{,}852 \\ -\ 8{,}402 \end{array}$ 6) $\begin{array}{r} 19{,}439 \\ -\ 9{,}829 \end{array}$ 7) $\begin{array}{r} 12{,}555 \\ -\ 5{,}004 \end{array}$ 8) $\begin{array}{r} 11{,}593 \\ -\ 8{,}454 \end{array}$

	A	B	C	D
E				
F				
G				
H				

Clues

A. All of the digits are odd.
B. The first digit is even and less than 5.
C. The second and third digits are equal.
D. The sum of the digits is 10.
E. The last digit is 8.
F. The first digit is 1.
G. The sum of the digits is 12.
H. The number is even and greater than 9,000.

Follow the same instructions for this puzzle. Be careful—it has only three clues.

9) $\begin{array}{r} 34{,}259 \\ -\ 24{,}941 \end{array}$ 10) $\begin{array}{r} 15{,}031 \\ -\ 11{,}390 \end{array}$ 11) $\begin{array}{r} 10{,}014 \\ -\ 2{,}519 \end{array}$ 12) $\begin{array}{r} 9{,}856 \\ -\ 7{,}683 \end{array}$

13) $\begin{array}{r} 15{,}342 \\ -\ 9{,}711 \end{array}$ 14) $\begin{array}{r} 11{,}916 \\ -\ 2{,}344 \end{array}$ 15) $\begin{array}{r} 7{,}378 \\ -\ 5{,}981 \end{array}$ 16) $\begin{array}{r} 16{,}866 \\ -\ 8{,}713 \end{array}$

	A	B	C	D
E				
F				
G				
H				

Clues

A. The sum of the digits is 23.
E. The number is divisible by 3.
G. The number is divisible by 5.

Mystery Numbers

Name _____ Date _____

1 I am a number less than 40. One of my factors is 7. The sum of my digits is 8.

What number am I? _____

2 I am a number less than 100. Two of my factors are 3 and 5. My digits are 1 apart.

What number am I? _____

3 I am a number less than 60. Two of my factors are 2 and 7. I am a common multiple of 8 and 14.

What number am I? _____

4 I am a common multiple of 2 and 5. I am also a factor of 100. The sum of my digits is 5.

What number am I? _____

5 I am a factor of 120, and a common multiple of 3, 4, and 10. The sum of my digits is 6.

What number am I? _____

6 I am a 2-digit number greater than 50. One of my factors is 8 and I, myself, am a factor of 360. The difference between my digits is 5.

What number am I? _____

Brain Power

Name _____ Date _____

1 The Eggplant Avenue bus passes Max's house every 8 minutes. The Cabbage Creek bus passes it every 12 minutes. The two buses last passed by together at 9:00 a.m.

When is the next time that will happen? _____

2 The Allentown train passes every 20 minutes. The Bard train passes every 15 minutes. The Carlton train passes every 18 minutes. It is 6:00 p.m., and all three just passed by.

When is the next time that will happen? _____

3 I am the fewest number of armadillos that meets the following conditions: When grouped by twos, by threes, or by fours, there is one left over. When grouped by fives, there are none left over.

What number am I? _____

4 I am the fewest number of fish that meets the following conditions: When netted by threes, by fours, or by fives, there is one left over.

What number am I? _____

Dr. Dee Vision's Famous Crossword

Name _____ Date _____

Do the division problems at the bottom of the page, and place the answers in the crossword puzzle.

Across

A. $28{,}060 \div 46 = $ _____

B. $12{,}644 \div 29 = $ _____

D. $27{,}126 \div 33 = $ _____

F. $12{,}499 \div 29 = $ _____

H. $75{,}502 \div 14 = $ _____

J. $32{,}650 \div 25 = $ _____

K. $79{,}128 \div 18 = $ _____

Down

A. $15{,}824 \div 23 = $ _____

B. $31{,}552 \div 64 = $ _____

C. $17{,}775 \div 25 = $ _____

E. $12{,}155 \div 11 = $ _____

G. $81{,}432 \div 27 = $ _____

I. $51{,}728 \div 16 = $ _____

J. $33{,}980 \div 20 = $ _____

Perfect Products

Name _____ Date _____

Choose one number from the triangle and one from the circle to answer each question. (Hint: Use division to help you!)

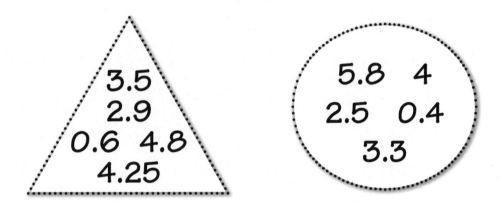

3.5
2.9
0.6 4.8
4.25

5.8 4
2.5 0.4
3.3

 1 Two numbers have a product of 8.75.

What are the numbers? _____

 2 Two numbers have a product of 17.

What are the numbers? _____

 3 Two numbers have a product that is less than 1.

What are the numbers? _____

 4 Two numbers have a product that is greater than 25.

What are the numbers? _____

Shoemaker

Name _____   Date _____

Why did the shoemaker quit her job? _____

To find the answer, solve the problems on page 21. Then plot the ordered pairs and connect the points. The picture you make will help you solve the riddle.

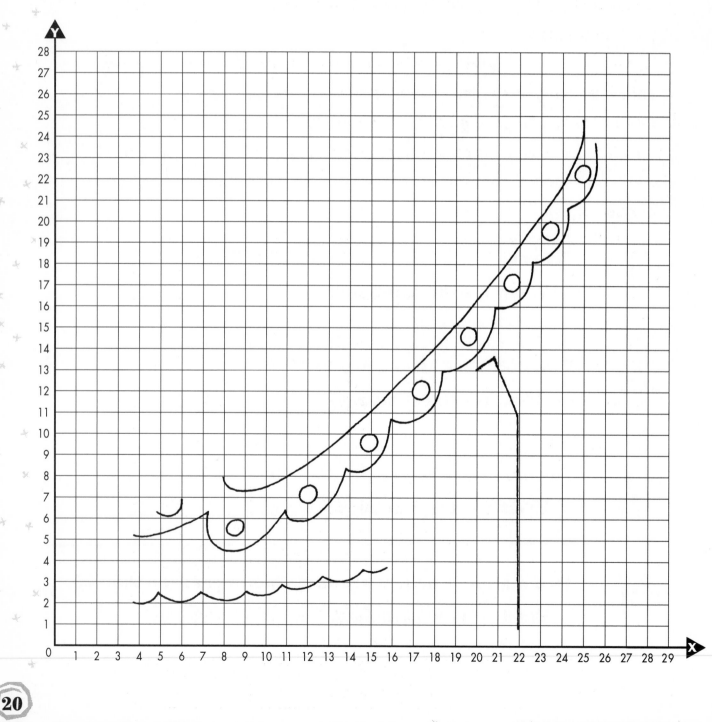

Shoemaker

Name _____ Date _____

1. Look at number 1, below. The number in the first column is the X coordinate in an ordered pair.

2. On a separate sheet of paper, solve the problem in the second column. Rename the answer in lowest terms. The numerator in the answer is the Y coordinate.

3. Write the X and Y coordinates in the third column to make an ordered pair. The first one has been done for you.

4. Determine the ordered pairs for the rest of the chart.

5. Plot the ordered pairs on the graph on page 20 in the order they are given. Then use a straightedge to connect the points in the order you plotted them. Can you solve the riddle?

	X Coordinate	Y Coordinate	Ordered Pair
1.	24	$3\frac{16}{27} + 2\frac{1}{3} = 5\frac{25}{27}$	(24, 25)
2.	25	$7\frac{5}{32} + 4\frac{5}{8} =$	
3.	27	$6\frac{3}{5} + 3\frac{6}{25} =$	
4.	27	$2\frac{3}{15} + 2\frac{11}{30} =$	
5.	24	$6\frac{10}{36} + 2\frac{6}{18} =$	
6.	24	$1\frac{1}{5} + 1\frac{2}{10} =$	
7.	22	$5\frac{2}{18} + 1\frac{1}{9} =$	
8.	21	$1\frac{1}{8} + 2\frac{1}{4} =$	
9.	21	$1\frac{6}{38} + 4\frac{7}{19} =$	
10.	20	$3\frac{18}{42} + 4\frac{7}{14} =$	
11.	15	$4\frac{2}{30} + 2\frac{1}{15} =$	
12.	8	$1\frac{4}{9} + 1\frac{1}{18} =$	
13.	4	$7\frac{2}{7} + 7\frac{3}{14} =$	
14.	3	$2\frac{1}{9} + 3\frac{1}{3} =$	
15.	4	$2\frac{6}{14} + 1\frac{3}{7} =$	
16.	8	$8\frac{3}{25} + 9\frac{1}{5} =$	
17.	24	$11\frac{22}{82} + 8\frac{14}{41} =$	

Fraction Flowers

Name _____ Date _____

Place one fraction from the box into each flower petal. Every petal should contain a fraction that is equivalent to the fraction in the center of the flower. Be careful, there are three fractions that will not be used.

$\frac{7}{14}$	$\frac{2}{18}$	$\frac{20}{30}$	$\frac{27}{36}$	$\frac{30}{40}$	$\frac{14}{16}$	$\frac{4}{6}$	$\frac{21}{24}$	$\frac{6}{12}$
$\frac{33}{44}$	$\frac{70}{80}$	$\frac{15}{20}$	$\frac{10}{20}$	$\frac{5}{30}$	$\frac{9}{18}$	$\frac{6}{9}$	$\frac{63}{72}$	$\frac{77}{88}$
$\frac{33}{66}$	$\frac{12}{18}$	$\frac{50}{75}$	$\frac{12}{24}$	$\frac{35}{40}$	$\frac{75}{100}$	$\frac{2}{9}$	$\frac{6}{8}$	$\frac{34}{51}$

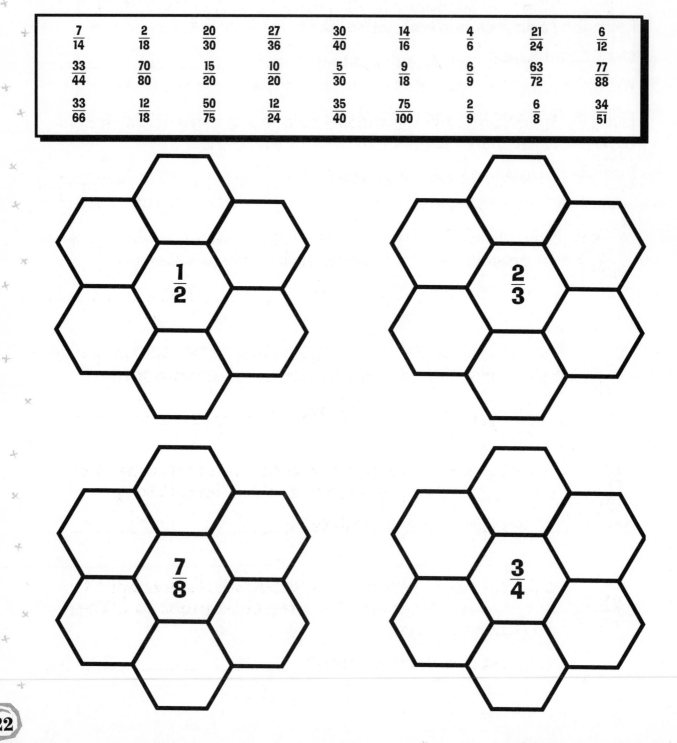

Find the Fractions

Name _____ Date _____

To solve these puzzlers, you may use
numbers more than once.

 Use the numbers 3, 12, and 6 to create two fractions that are equivalent to $\frac{1}{2}$.

What are the fractions? _____

 Use two prime numbers to create a fraction that is equivalent to $\frac{21}{49}$.

What is the fraction? _____

 Use the numbers 3 and 12 and one other whole number to create two fractions that are equivalent to $\frac{1}{4}$.

What are the fractions? _____

 Use the numbers 9 and 15 and one other whole number to create two fractions that are equivalent to $\frac{3}{5}$.

What are the fractions? _____

 Use the number 8 and two other whole numbers to create two fractions that are equivalent to $\frac{2}{3}$.

What are the fractions? _____

 Use the number 4 and two other whole numbers to create two fractions that are equivalent to $\frac{1}{2}$. Then do it another way.

What are the fractions? _____

Master Maze

Name _____ Date _____

If you're an expert at tunneling through mazes, this master maze is for you. Here's how to begin. Work through the maze and do not cross over your original path. As you pass each fraction, find it in reduced form in the data bank and cross it out. Continue until all of the fractions in the data bank have been located, then exit.

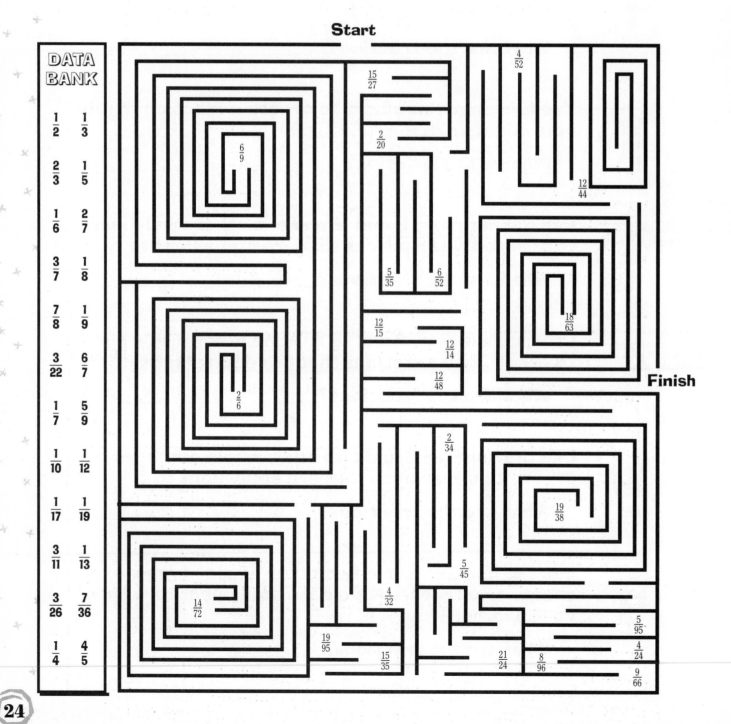

Match Maker

Name _____ Date _____

Rewrite fractions as decimals. To do this, divide the numerator by the denominator. Round to the nearest hundredth.

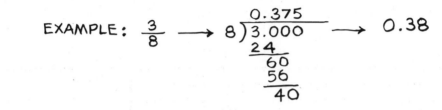

EXAMPLE: $\frac{3}{8}$ → $8\overline{)3.000}$ → 0.38

$$
\begin{array}{r}
0.375 \\
8\overline{)3.000} \\
\underline{24} \\
60 \\
\underline{56} \\
40
\end{array}
$$

1. $\frac{1}{4} =$	2. $\frac{3}{12} =$		3. $\frac{23}{1} =$	4. $\frac{12}{16}$
5. $\frac{6}{100} =$		6. $\frac{3}{5} =$	7. $\frac{2}{9} =$	8. $\frac{7}{16}$
9. $\frac{8}{9} =$	10. $\frac{6}{8} =$	11. $\frac{2}{3} =$	12. $\frac{45}{100} =$	
	13. $\frac{9}{12} =$	14. $\frac{23}{5} =$	15. $\frac{5}{8} =$	16. $\frac{4}{9} =$
17. $\frac{14}{16} =$	18. $\frac{7}{20} =$	19. $\frac{9}{8} =$		20. $\frac{5}{4} =$

Square Madness

Name _____ Date _____

Compare the decimals and write the larger decimal in the puzzle. The decimal point will occupy one space. Each number can occupy only one place to make the whole puzzle fit together perfectly. Two numbers have been given to get you started.

9.09 $<$ 9.18   18.3 $>$ 18.03   31.8 ◯ 30.4   54.1 ◯ 54

0.8 ◯ 0.82   29.5 ◯ 28.5   3.57 ◯ 3.55   8.31 ◯ 8.30

6.71 ◯ 6.75   41.05 ◯ 41.5   0.009 ◯ 0.09   5.20 ◯ 5.10

1.09 ◯ 1.08   9.33 ◯ 9.36   21.45 ◯ 21.5   3.22 ◯ 3.12

7.91 ◯ 7.90   0.102 ◯ 0.12   0.73 ◯ 0.71   93.4 ◯ 93.0

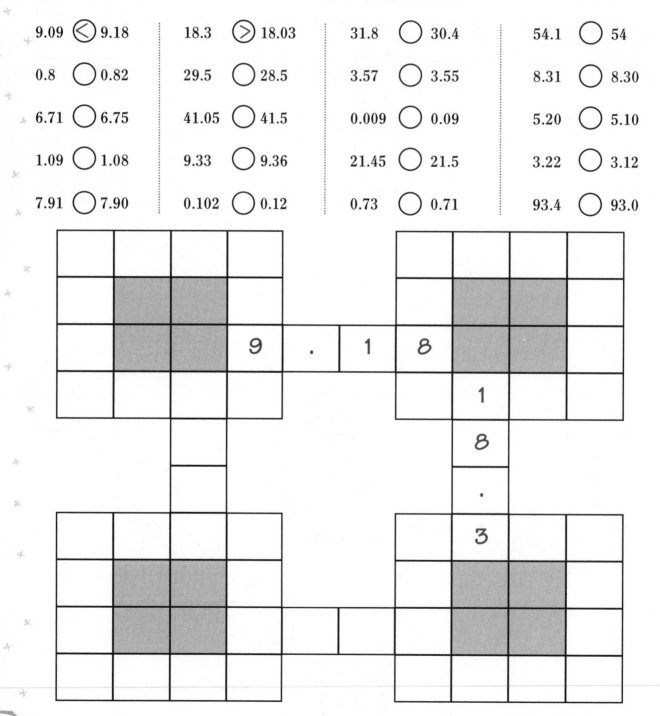

Magic Square

Name _____ Date _____

These squares are magic because each row of four circles magically adds up to 100. You're the magician. See if you can use the numbers in the box below to make the puzzle work. Four numbers have been added to get you started.

| 10.39 | 9.02 | 29 | 3.09 | 43 | 10.6 | 12.42 | 57.5 |

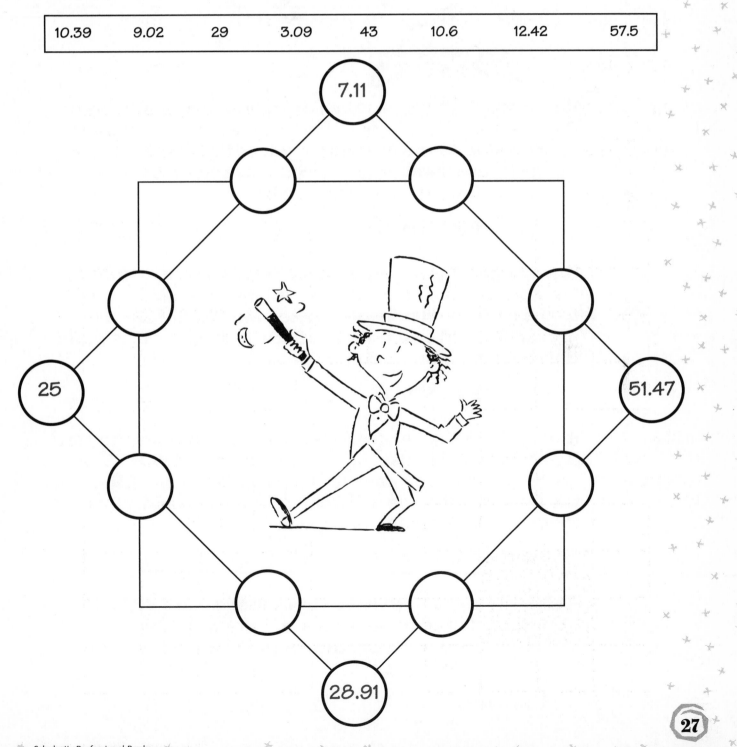

Round Decimals

Name _____ Date _____

1 Rounding to the nearest whole number makes me 4. Rounding to the nearest tenth makes me 4.2. When I am rounded to the nearest hundredth, I am 4.23. I am the greatest number carried out to the thousandths place that meets all these conditions.

What number am I? _____

2 Rounding to the nearest whole number makes me 13. Rounding to the nearest tenth makes me 12.6. Rounding to the nearest hundredth makes me 12.58. I am the greatest number carried out to the thousandths place that meets all these conditions.

What number am I? _____

3 Rounding to the nearest whole number makes me 115. Rounding to the nearest tenth makes me 114.9. When I am rounded to the nearest hundredth, I am 114.93. I am the least number carried out to the thousandths place that meets all these conditions.

What number am I? _____

4 Rounding to the nearest tenth makes me 203.5. Rounding to the nearest hundredth makes me 203.46. The sum of my digits is 15. Carry me out to the thousandths place.

What number am I? _____

28

Dialing for Answers

Name _____ Date _____

How much does an elephant charge for a circus performance?
Find out the answer by solving each puzzle and replacing the number in
the ones place with the letter from the telephone code. Then write the
letters on the dotted lines. The first one has been done for you.

1.
$$13.7 \times 8 = 109.6 \quad \text{P}$$

2.
$$13.2 \times 4$$
___

3.
$$37.5 \times 12$$
___

4.
$$19.11 \times 18$$
___

5.
$$21.03 \times 24$$
___

6.
$$46.4 \times 6$$
___

7.
$$30.45 \times 15$$
___

| 1 | 2 | 3 | 4 | 5 | 6 | 7 |

Telephone keypad:
1 A, 2 E, 3 N
4 U, 5 C, 6 S
7 R, 8 T, 9 P
* M, 0 A, # R

What weighs more than a ton and carries a trunk wherever it goes?

8.
$$2.35 \times 5$$
___

9.
$$64.2 \times 6$$
___

10.
$$45.8 \times 2$$
___

11.
$$35.15 \times 15$$
___

| 8 | 9 | 10 | 11 |

29

Rate Creator

Name _____ Date _____

A rate is a fraction that expresses two different units of measure.
Complete the rate chart below.

1. HUMAN HEART BEATS

HEARTBEATS	84					
MINUTES	1	2	3	4	5	6

2. WORDS READ

WORDS	55					
MINUTE	1	2	3	6	10	15

3. CAR MILES TRAVELED

MILES	50					
HOUR	1	2	3	4	5	6

4. COST OF PARKING

COST	$2.75					
HOUR	1	2	3	4	5	6

5. MILES TRAVELED BY CAR

MILES	35					
GALLON	1	5	10	15	30	60

6. DOLLARS EARNED

DOLLARS	$6.50					
HOURS	1	2	3	4	6	8

7. COMPUTER TYPING

WORDS	42					
MINUTES	1	2	3	5	10	15

8. CANDY KISSES

COST	18¢					
OUNCES	1	3	8	12	14	16

9. BABYSITTING

COST	$4					
HOUR	1	2	3	4	5	6

10. MOVIE CAMERA

FRAMES	24					
SECOND	1	30	60	120	240	480

I can type 400 words a minute with lots of mistakes.

Brain Rattler

Name _____ Date _____

Ready for a brain-rattling number game? Cut out the game pieces from around the game board and place them on the game board in the order shown in the box at the bottom of the page. Then, move the game pieces until each horizontal row has an equivalent decimal, percent, and fraction (in lowest terms). You may move only one piece at a time into the empty circle. You may move vertically, horizontally, or diagonally.

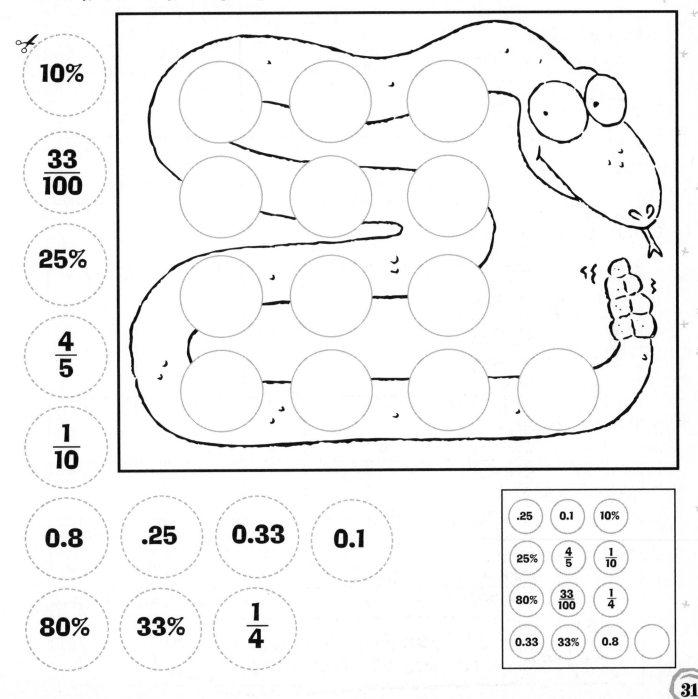

Scholastic Professional Books

Convertor Clerk

Name _____ Date _____

Find 10 fraction/decimal/percent equivalents in this grid. They appear together in a row across and down and backwards. Hint: Fraction $(\frac{15}{100})$ = decimal (0.15) = percent (15%).

87%	87.5	$\frac{7}{8}$	.875	$87\frac{1}{2}$%	.24	24%
$\frac{25}{100}$	$\frac{3}{5}$	50%	$\frac{12}{5}$	2.4	240%	$\frac{6}{20}$
0.25	.03	.50	$\frac{7}{25}$	$\frac{1}{5}$	.20	20%
25%	30%	$\frac{2}{4}$	.27	$\frac{6}{8}$	0.75	75%
$\frac{1}{8}$	0.125	12.5%	27%	.27	$\frac{10}{25}$	2.5
70%	$\frac{18}{40}$	.45	45%	$\frac{2}{4}$	.40	40%
0.7	$\frac{112}{200}$	1.12	112%	$\frac{11}{112}$	40%	.405
$\frac{4}{5}$	.0625	62.5%	62%	$\frac{7}{25}$	.28	28%

Family Reunion Picnic

Name _____   Date _____

You Answer It!

1. What was the ratio of grandparents to uncles at the picnic? Write your answer in lowest terms.

_____

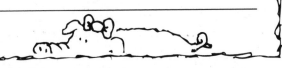

Write all ratios in lowest terms.

2. What was the ratio of uncles to cousins at the picnic? _____

3. Eight of the cousins at the picnic were boys. How many of the cousins were girls? What was the ratio of girl cousins to boy cousins? _____

4. What was the ratio of boy cousins to all cousins at the picnic? _____

5. What was the ratio of girl cousins to uncles at the picnic? _____

6. What was the ratio of grandparents to cousins and uncles? _____

7. What was the ratio of ants to all others at the picnic? _____

8. Ten percent or 10 out of every 100 ants were red. How many of the ants at the picnic were red? _____

9. Four hundred of the 800 ants were late to the picnic. What percent of the ants were late? _____

WRAP IT UP! Seventy percent or 70 out of every 100 ants at the picnic were hungry. How many of the ants were not hungry?

_____

33

Number Jumper

Name _____ Date _____

A related or continued series is called a sequence. Write the next three numbers in these sequences.

1.
0, 3, 8, 15, _____

2.
9, 17, 25, 41, 57, _____

3.
128, 64, 32, 16, _____

4.
100, 81, 64, 49, _____

5.
95, 91, 87, 83, _____

6.
2, 8, 32, 128, _____

7.
60, 57, 53, 48, _____

8.
30, 27, 24, 21, _____

9.
4, 12, 20, 28, _____

10.
1, 3, 5, 7, _____

11.
1, 4, 8, 13, _____

12.
$\frac{1}{2}$, $\frac{2}{3}$, $\frac{3}{4}$, $\frac{4}{5}$, _____

13.
3, 4, 7, 11, _____

14.
1, 2, 3, 5, 8, _____

15.
4, 8, 12, 16, _____

16.
$\frac{2}{3}$, $\frac{4}{5}$, $\frac{6}{7}$, $\frac{8}{9}$, _____

17.
1, 3, 9, 27, 81, _____

18.
2, 4, 7, 11, _____

Pattern Finder

Name _____ Date _____

Patterns are fun! Think about patterns as you answer these questions.

1. The numbers 36, 45, and 54 are all divisible by 9. Write more numbers that are divisible by 9. _____
   Look at the numbers. Write a rule for identifying when a number is divisible by 9. _____

2. Here is a way to check if a number is divisible by 3: a. add up all the digits in the number; b. If the sum is a number that is divisible by 3, then the original number is divisible by 3. Complete the chart below.

NO.	SUM OF DIGITS	DIVISIBLE BY 3?	CHECK
54	5+4 =9	YES	54÷3=18
132			
516			
711			
333			

3. Presidential elections are held every 4 years. The first election of the 21st century was in November, 2000. Between 2000 and 2035, which years will be presidential election years? _____

4. Use the Roman numeral chart to decipher the value of the following numerals.
   CLXV _____ MCMXCIX _____
   DCCCII _____

```
ROMAN NUMERAL CHART
1 I      6 VI      50 L
2 II     7 VII     100 C
3 III    8 VIII    500 D
4 IV     9 IX      900 CM
5 V     10 X      1000 M
```

5. Write your phone number using Roman numerals. (Think of your phone number as 7 different digits.)

_____

Coin Problems

Name _____   Date _____

 1 Anna has 15 coins in her purse. All are nickels and dimes. They total $1.35.

How many of each does she have? _____

 2 Royce has $1.30 in dimes and quarters. He has one-fourth as many quarters as dimes.

How many of each does he have? _____

 3 Letty has $5 in nickels, dimes, and quarters. She has 3 times as many nickels as dimes. She has 5 times as much money in quarters as she does in nickels.

How many of each does she have? _____

 4 Five dollars is divided continuously among three boys. The first boy always gets $.02, the second boy always gets $.03, and the third always gets $.05, until all the money is gone.

How much money does each boy get? _____

Real Dealer

Name _____ Date _____

Hanlon's flower catalog and Murray's flower catalog are having sales of flower bulbs. Write the price per bulb. Then circle the better buy.

	HANLON'S		Murray's
1.	5 for $6.99	OR	6 for $5.49
2.	54 for $16.47	OR	42 for $15.99
3.	18 for $10.98	OR	12 for $9.98
4.	53 for $29.00	OR	60 for $35.00
5.	28 for $15.98	OR	25 for $10.99
6.	50 for $19.98	OR	45 for $17.29
7.	40 for $19.48	OR	48 for $14.98
8.	80 for $29.99	OR	96 for $28.96

	HANLON'S	MURRAY'S
1.	_____	_____
2.	_____	_____
3.	_____	_____
4.	_____	_____
5.	_____	_____
6.	_____	_____
7.	_____	_____
8.	_____	_____

I planted light bulbs to get brighter flowers.

A Bear in Full

Name _____ Date _____

Figure It Out!

1. Monica Bear's new mirror measures 72 inches by 60 inches. What is the perimeter of the mirror? (Perimeter is the distance all the way around.)

_____

2. Another mirror is shaped like a square. That means that all 4 sides are the same length. The mirror's perimeter is 24 inches. How long is each side? _____

3. Ant Betty's full-length mirror is 3 1/2 inches across and 4 1/2 inches down. What is its perimeter? _____

4. Which has a greater perimeter, a mirror that measures 8 1/2 inches across and 12 inches down or a mirror that measures 12 1/2 inches across and 8 inches down?

_____

5. Mirror A measures 5 inches across and 7 inches down. Mirror B measures 8 inches across and 3 inches down. Which mirror's perimeter is bigger? How much bigger?

_____

SUPER CHALLENGE: A mirror is shaped like a rectangle. Its width is twice as long as its height. The mirror is 11 inches high. What is its width? What is the mirror's perimeter? _____

Scholastic Success With Math: Grade 6

Shape Gaper

Name _____ Date _____

FLAT SHAPES HAVE LENGTH AND WIDTH.

A SQUARE   B CIRCLE   C RECTANGLE   D TRIANGLE

SOLID SHAPES HAVE LENGTH AND WIDTH AND DEPTH.

E CUBE   F SPHERE   G CYLINDER   H CONE   I RECTANGULAR PRISM   J PYRAMID

MATCH THE SHAPES WITH THESE OBJECTS. USE THE LETTERS ABOVE.

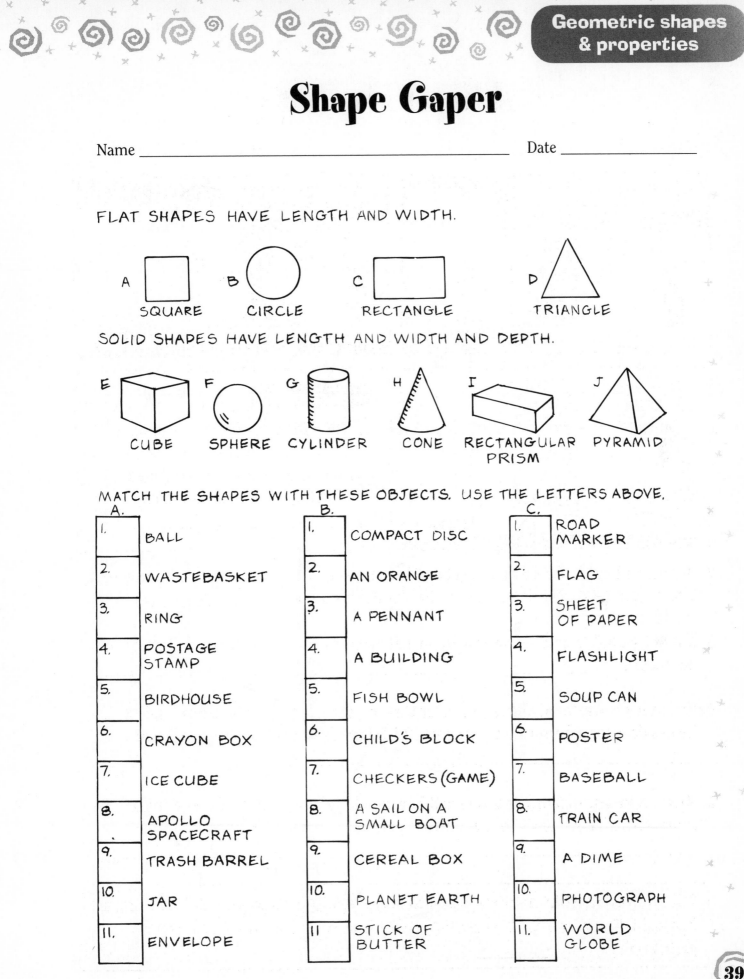

A.
1.	BALL
2.	WASTEBASKET
3.	RING
4.	POSTAGE STAMP
5.	BIRDHOUSE
6.	CRAYON BOX
7.	ICE CUBE
8.	APOLLO SPACECRAFT
9.	TRASH BARREL
10.	JAR
11.	ENVELOPE

B.
1.	COMPACT DISC
2.	AN ORANGE
3.	A PENNANT
4.	A BUILDING
5.	FISH BOWL
6.	CHILD'S BLOCK
7.	CHECKERS (GAME)
8.	A SAIL ON A SMALL BOAT
9.	CEREAL BOX
10.	PLANET EARTH
11	STICK OF BUTTER

C.
1.	ROAD MARKER
2.	FLAG
3.	SHEET OF PAPER
4.	FLASHLIGHT
5.	SOUP CAN
6.	POSTER
7.	BASEBALL
8.	TRAIN CAR
9.	A DIME
10.	PHOTOGRAPH
11.	WORLD GLOBE

Shape Finder

Hidden in the puzzle are 5 kinds of quadrilaterals (4-sided polygons). Find them and initial them with a pencil so that they can be easily identified.

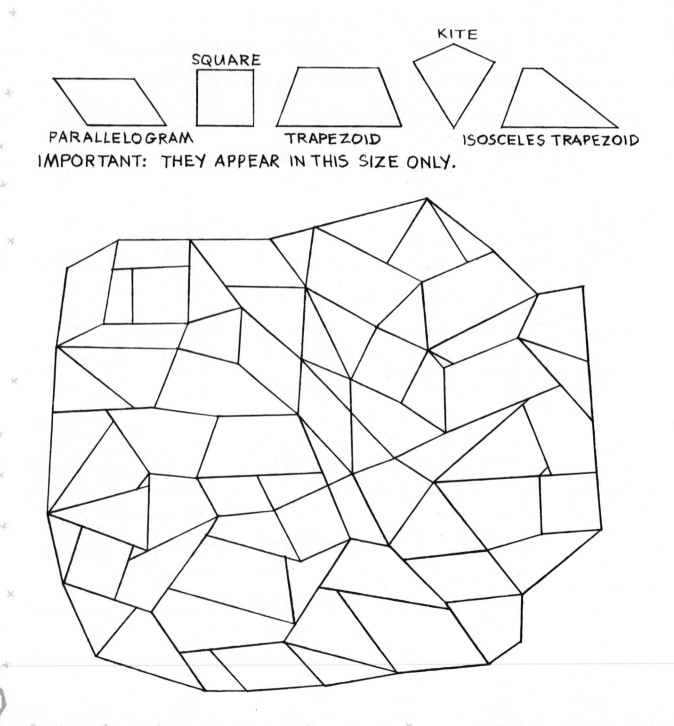

KITE

SQUARE

PARALLELOGRAM

TRAPEZOID

ISOSCELES TRAPEZOID

IMPORTANT: THEY APPEAR IN THIS SIZE ONLY.

Quick Cubes

Name _____ Date _____

1 **Twenty-seven small cubes are stacked to make this block. The entire block is painted red.**

   How many cubes are painted on one side? _____

   How many cubes are painted on two sides? _____

   How many cubes are painted on three sides? _____

   How many cubes are unpainted? _____

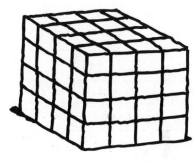

2 **Sixty-four small cubes are stacked to make this block. The entire block is painted blue.**

   How many cubes are painted on one side? _____

   How many of the cubes are unpainted? _____

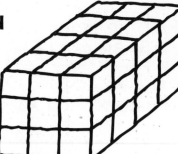

3 **Thirty-six small cubes are stacked to make this rectangular prism. The whole prism is painted green.**

   How many cubes are painted on three sides? _____

   How many cubes are unpainted? _____

Great Decorator

Name _____ Date _____

Find the cost per square foot for these home-improvement materials, indoors and out. Hint: Length x width = sq. foot x cost of material = price.

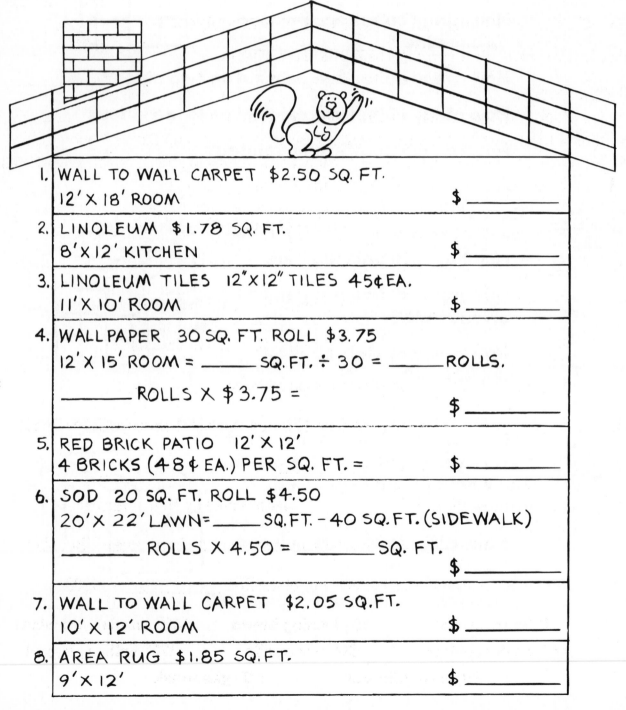

1. WALL TO WALL CARPET $2.50 SQ. FT.
   12' X 18' ROOM $ _____

2. LINOLEUM $1.78 SQ. FT.
   8' X 12' KITCHEN $ _____

3. LINOLEUM TILES 12" X 12" TILES 45¢ EA.
   11' X 10' ROOM $ _____

4. WALLPAPER 30 SQ. FT. ROLL $3.75
   12' X 15' ROOM = _____ SQ. FT. ÷ 30 = _____ ROLLS.
   _____ ROLLS X $ 3.75 =
                                                     $ _____

5. RED BRICK PATIO 12' X 12'
   4 BRICKS (48¢ EA.) PER SQ. FT. = $ _____

6. SOD 20 SQ. FT. ROLL $4.50
   20' X 22' LAWN = _____ SQ. FT. – 40 SQ. FT. (SIDEWALK)
   _____ ROLLS X 4.50 = _____ SQ. FT.
                                                     $ _____

7. WALL TO WALL CARPET $2.05 SQ. FT.
   10' X 12' ROOM $ _____

8. AREA RUG $1.85 SQ. FT.
   9' X 12' $ _____

Get an "Angle" on Inventions

Name _____ Date _____

✎ Everything that people use in their daily lives was invented by some-one—things like the ironing board, the cash register, and ear muffs. In this activity, we ask you to match inventions such as these to their inventor. Follow the directions below to get a new "angle" on a few famous inventions.

40°

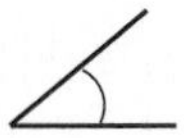

90°

180°

DIRECTIONS:
• Take a look at the angle that appears before each statement.
• Estimate the measure of the angle in degrees using the 40°, 90°, and 180° angles as a guide.
• Next, circle the name of the invention that appears next to the best estimate of that angle.
• Write the correct invention in the space provided in the statement.

1.  The _____ was invented in 1888 by A.B. Blackburn.

2. 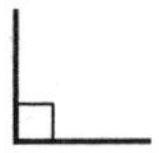 S. Boone invented the _____ in 1892.

3. 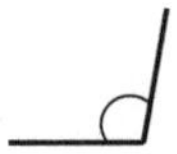 The _____ was invented in 1912 by Garrett A. Morgan.

4.  The _____ was invented in 1879 by James Ritty.

5.  In 1877, Chester Greenwood invented _____.

6.  In 1935, Laszlo and Georg Biro established themselves as the first

inventors of the _____.

7.  In 1902, the _____ was invented by Miller Hutchison.

8.  Other inventors expanded on her invention in later years. But Mary

Anderson was the inventor of the first _____ in 1903.

11° hearing aid	90° ironing board	130° windshield wiper
160° cash register	80° ear muffs	175° railway signal
20° ballpoint pen	110° gas mask	

43

Multiple Measures

Name _____ Date _____

Circle the correct answer for each problem.

1. The library is located on Peale Street. Which street is perpendicular to Peale Street?
   a. Broadway
   b. Clark Street
   c. Sharp Street
   d. Allen Street

2. The floor in the library's rectangular lobby is 28 feet long and 16 feet wide. What is the area of the floor?
   a. 44 ft²   c. 224 ft²
   b. 88 ft²   d. 448 ft²

3. Sophie made some folded paper figures for the art show. In which figure is the dotted line a line of symmetry?

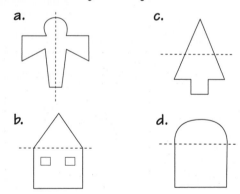

4. Keith made a metal sculpture in the shape of a triangular prism. How many faces does the prism have?
   a. 3   c. 6
   b. 5   d. 8

5. The courtyard at the library is a square measuring 18 yards on one side. What is the perimeter of the courtyard?
   a. 36 yd   c. 72 yd
   b. 54 yd   d. 324 yd

6. Devon made this sign in the shape of a right triangle. What is the area of the sign?

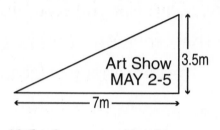

   a. 10.5 m²   c. 14 m²
   b. 12.25 m²   d. 24.5 m²

7. Cleo's art project was a cylinder made of recycled plastic. Which of these could be Cleo's project?

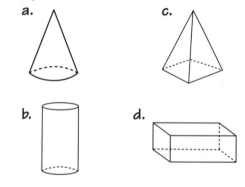

8. Manuel made a clear plastic box and filled it with colored shapes. What is the volume of the box Manuel made?

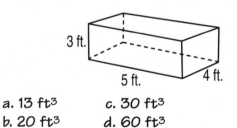

   a. 13 ft³   c. 30 ft³
   b. 20 ft³   d. 60 ft³

Alert Convertor

Name _____ Date _____

Convert small units of measure to large units. Example: inches into feet ➔ 12 in. = 1 ft. ➔ total inches in the first problem below ÷ 12 = number of feet. Use the chart for reference.

12 in. = 1 ft.	7 days = 1 week
32 oz. = 1 qt.	36 in. = 1 yd.
8 oz. = 1 cup	12 units = 1 doz.
60 min. = 1 hr.	16 oz. = 1 lb.
8 pts. = 1 gal.	

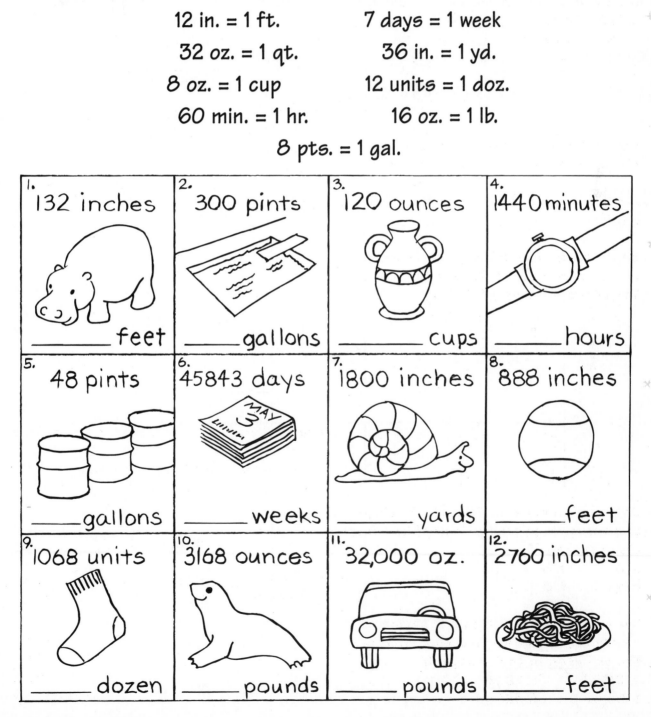

1. 132 inches _____ feet

2. 300 pints _____ gallons

3. 120 ounces _____ cups

4. 1440 minutes _____ hours

5. 48 pints _____ gallons

6. 45843 days _____ weeks

7. 1800 inches _____ yards

8. 888 inches _____ feet

9. 1068 units _____ dozen

10. 3168 ounces _____ pounds

11. 32,000 oz. _____ pounds

12. 2760 inches _____ feet

Bedtime for Baby

Name _____ Date _____

Riddle: What do baby sweet potatoes sleep in?

Use the coordinates to identify points on the graph. Then use the point names to solve the riddle by filling in the blanks at the bottom of the page.

❶ (2,1) _____   ❻ (2,-5) _____

❷ (3,5) _____   ❼ (-2,2) _____

❸ (4,-2) _____   ❽ (-3,5) _____

❹ (5,0) _____   ❾ (4,-4) _____

❺ (1,-3) _____   ❿ (-4,-2) _____

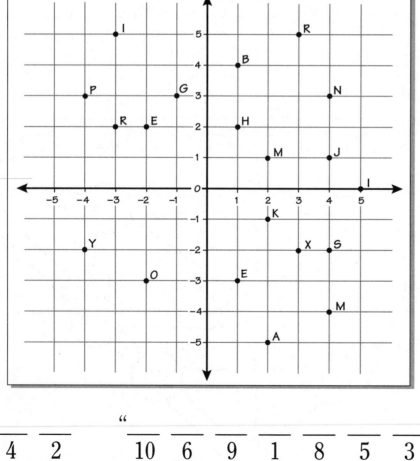

TH ___ ___ ___ " ___ ___ ___ ___ ___ ___ ___ ___ "
    7   4   2   10   6   9   1   8   5   3

Galactic Math

Name _____ Date _____

Find your way through the Islandic Labyrinth. Begin your journey at the top. Move along the paths from one circle to the next, performing the operation indicated. For instance:

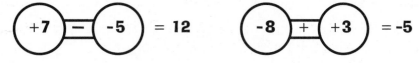

$(+7) - (-5) = 12$ $(-8) + (+3) = -5$

Tally your score as you go. You may never retrace your path or cross over it. When you get to the exit, if your score is 19, you may exit. If not, try again.

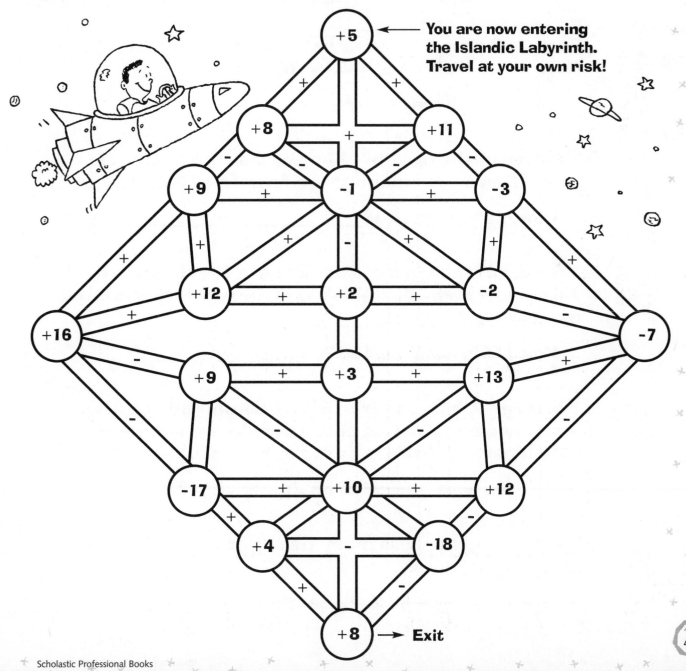

You are now entering the Islandic Labyrinth. Travel at your own risk!

Exit

Age Equations

Name _____ Date _____

1 Patty is 3 times as old as her brother, Terry. In 10 years, the sum of their ages will be 36.

How old are they now? _____

2 The sum of the ages of Mike and Dan is 20 years. In 4 years, Dan's age will be three-fourths of Mike's age.

How old is Mike now? _____

3 The sum of the ages of Jasmine and her mother is 100. Thirty years ago, Jasmine's mother was 9 times as old as Jasmine was then.

How old is Jasmine now? _____

4 The three Athios children have a combined age of 50. The youngest is half as old as the oldest. Ten years ago, the oldest was 7 times as old as the youngest.

How old were the children 10 years ago? _____

5 Naomi caught half as many fish as Jack did. Together they caught 18 fish.

How many fish did Jack catch? _____

Don't Be Square

Name _____ Date _____

1 When the square root of one number is multiplied by the square root of a second number, the product is the square root of 36. One of the numbers is not 1.

What are the numbers? _____

2 When the square of one number is subtracted from the square of another, the difference is 1 less than the square of 9.

What are the numbers?

_____

3 The sum of the square and the positive square root of a number is 84.

What is the number?

_____

4 Two numbers are both less than the square of 10. One is the cube root of the other. When the positive square root of one of these numbers is added to the positive square root of the other number, the sum is the square root of a 3-digit number.

What are the numbers? _____

Exponent Experts Only

Name _____ Date _____

If you are experienced at finding exponents, this exercise is for you! Solve the problems, then use the clues in the puzzle to fit your answers in the correct spaces.

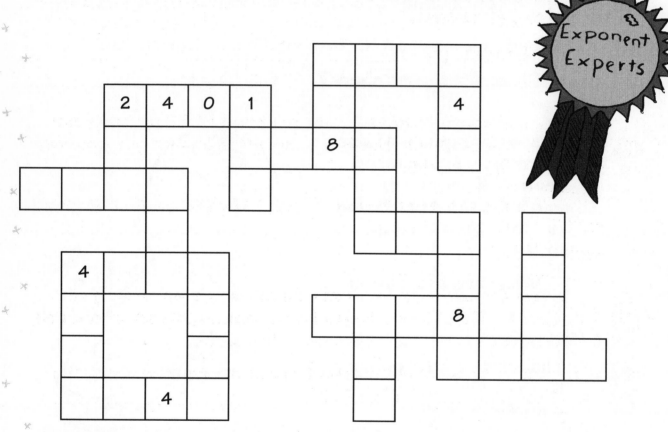

Find the product and write the answer in the puzzle. Each digit can occupy only one place to make the whole puzzle fit together perfectly. The first one has been done for you.

7^4 = _____2,401_____ 11^2 = _____ 3^6 = _____

3^7 = _____ 17^2 = _____ 13^3 = _____

43^2 = _____ 2^7 = _____ 3^6 = _____

95^2 = _____ 18^3 = _____ 31^2 = _____

33^2 = _____ 12^3 = _____ 19^3 = _____

27^2 = _____ 8^4 = _____ 69^2 = _____

21^2 = _____ 4^5 = _____

Grade Averages

Name _____   Date _____

1 Jenny's mean score on three science tests was 75. Her last two scores were 79 and 80. She forgot her score on the first test.

What was it? _____

2 Wanda wants to have a test average of 90 on her four French exams. On the first three tests, she got scores of 84, 96, and 85.

What does she need on the last test to reach her goal?

_____

3 In Dave's Latin class, tests count twice as heavily as quizzes. On the two tests he has taken, his scores were 70 and 85. He is taking a quiz this week.

What score does he need to get in order to bring his exam average up to 80? _____

4 Carla is in Dave's Latin class. On the two tests, she scored 80 and 86. After taking the quiz, her exam average was 85.

What score did she get on the quiz? _____

Nature Patterns

Name _____ Date _____

1 A big bug ate 54 smaller bugs in 4 days. Each day, it ate 5 more bugs than it did on the previous day.

How many small bugs did the big bug eat on ...

the first day? _____

the fourth day? _____

2 A huge frog ate 140 big bugs in 5 days. Each day, it ate 8 more bugs than it did on the previous day.

How many bugs did the frog eat on ...

the first day? _____

the fifth day? _____

3 A little bug ate 135 tiny flies in 5 days. Each day, it ate 10 more flies than it did on the previous day.

How many flies had the bug eaten ...

after three days? _____

after four days? _____

4 A cat pestered a mouse for the entire time the mouse lived in the basement: 6 days. Each day, it pestered the mouse 7 times more than it did the day before. In all, the cat annoyed the mouse 123 times.

How many times was the mouse pestered on the fourth day? _____

Highway Robbery

Name _____ Date _____

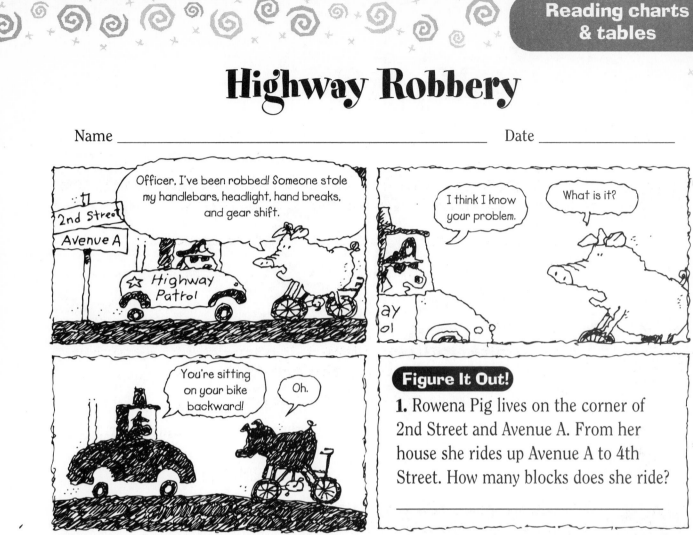

Figure It Out!

1. Rowena Pig lives on the corner of 2nd Street and Avenue A. From her house she rides up Avenue A to 4th Street. How many blocks does she ride?

_____

2. Rowena rides from the bank on 2nd Street and Avenue D to the bike shop on 5th Street and Avenue D. How many blocks does she ride? _____

3. Rowena rides up Avenue A from her house to the park on 5th Street and Avenue E. How many blocks does she ride? _____

4. Rowena rides up 4th Street from Avenue B to Avenue E. Then she turns around and rides back to Avenue A. How many blocks does she ride? _____

5. Rowena goes for a bike ride. She starts at 3rd Street and Avenue E. She rides to 3rd Street and Avenue B. Then she turns right to 2nd Street and Avenue B. How many blocks does she ride? _____

SUPER CHALLENGE: Rowena can go from her house to the bank by riding up 1st Street or by riding up 3rd Street. Which way is shorter?

53

Magic Show

Name _____   Date _____

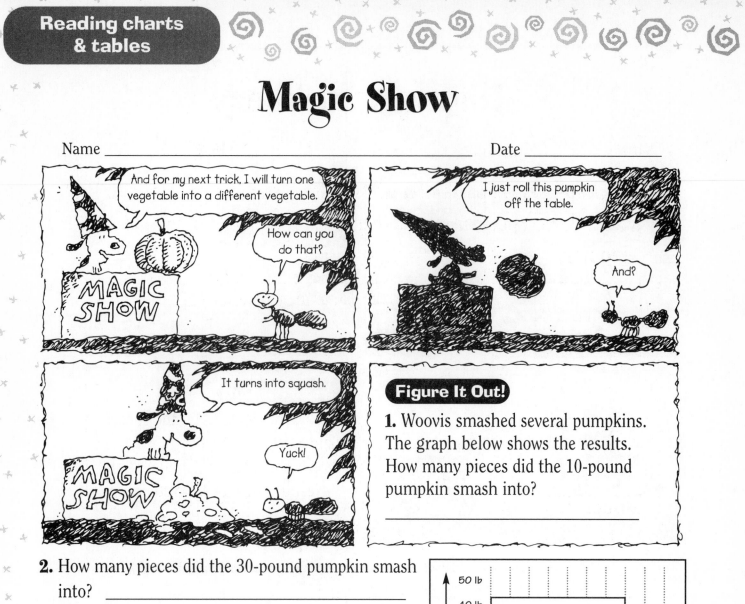

Figure It Out!

1. Woovis smashed several pumpkins. The graph below shows the results. How many pieces did the 10-pound pumpkin smash into?

_____

2. How many pieces did the 30-pound pumpkin smash into? _____

3. How many more pieces did the 40-pound pumpkin smash into than the 30-pound pumpkin?

_____

4. How many 10-pound pumpkins do you need to smash to get the same number of pieces in a 40-pound smashed pumpkin? _____

5. Look at the pattern on the graph. How many pieces would you expect a 50-pound pumpkin to smash into? Draw a bar on the graph. _____

SUPER CHALLENGE: How many pieces would you expect a 100-pound pumpkin to smash into?

Graph Drafter

Name _____ Date _____

A circle graph shows parts of a whole. Use these circle graphs to find out what people chose and how many. Hint: 36% ➔ .36 ➔ .36 x 220 = 72 people.

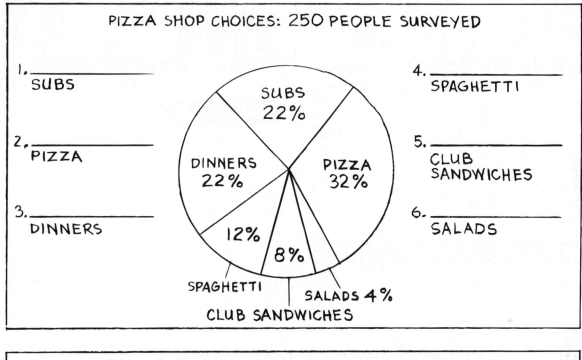

PIZZA SHOP CHOICES: 250 PEOPLE SURVEYED

1. _____ SUBS

2. _____ PIZZA

3. _____ DINNERS

4. _____ SPAGHETTI

5. _____ CLUB SANDWICHES

6. _____ SALADS

SUBS 22%
DINNERS 22%
PIZZA 32%
12%
8%
SPAGHETTI
SALADS 4%
CLUB SANDWICHES

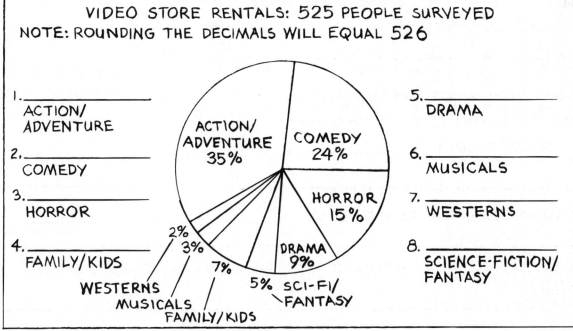

VIDEO STORE RENTALS: 525 PEOPLE SURVEYED
NOTE: ROUNDING THE DECIMALS WILL EQUAL 526

1. _____ ACTION/ ADVENTURE

2. _____ COMEDY

3. _____ HORROR

4. _____ FAMILY/KIDS

5. _____ DRAMA

6. _____ MUSICALS

7. _____ WESTERNS

8. _____ SCIENCE-FICTION/ FANTASY

ACTION/ ADVENTURE 35%
COMEDY 24%
HORROR 15%
2%
3%
7%
DRAMA 9%
5% SCI-FI/ FANTASY
WESTERNS
MUSICALS
FAMILY/KIDS

Doctor Knows Best

Name _____ Date _____

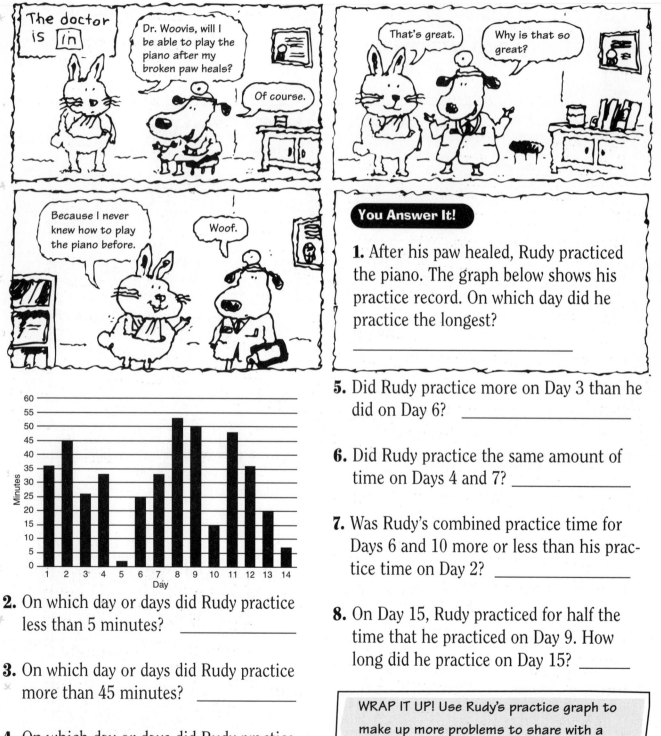

You Answer It!

1. After his paw healed, Rudy practiced
the piano. The graph below shows his
practice record. On which day did he
practice the longest?

_____

2. On which day or days did Rudy practice
less than 5 minutes? _____

3. On which day or days did Rudy practice
more than 45 minutes? _____

4. On which day or days did Rudy practice
between 10 and 20 minutes? _____

5. Did Rudy practice more on Day 3 than he
did on Day 6? _____

6. Did Rudy practice the same amount of
time on Days 4 and 7? _____

7. Was Rudy's combined practice time for
Days 6 and 10 more or less than his practice time on Day 2? _____

8. On Day 15, Rudy practiced for half the
time that he practiced on Day 9. How
long did he practice on Day 15? _____

WRAP IT UP! Use Rudy's practice graph to
make up more problems to share with a
friend.

A Riddle to Dive Into

Name _____ Date _____

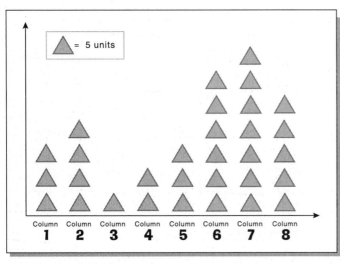

Riddle: How can you dive without getting wet?

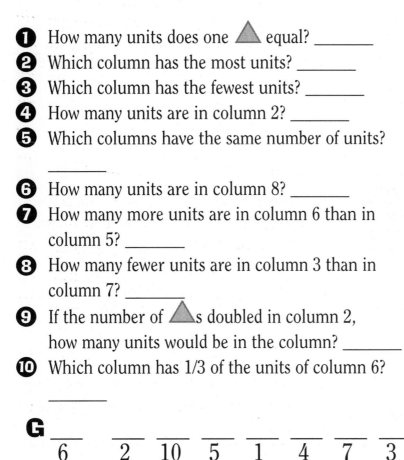

Decoder

40 units .... **G**

50 units .... **A**

column 7 .... **S**

column 1 .... **P**

column 4 .... **K**

30 units .... **N**

columns 2 and 8 .... **E**

25 units .... **O**

20 units .... **I**

column 6 .... **H**

35 units .... **W**

5 units .... **D**

15 units .... **V**

column 8 .... **T**

10 units .... **L**

column 3 .... **I**

columns 1 and 5 .... **Y**

Answer the questions about the graph. Then use the Decoder to solve the riddle by filling in the blanks at the bottom of the page.

❶ How many units does one ▲ equal? _____

❷ Which column has the most units? _____

❸ Which column has the fewest units? _____

❹ How many units are in column 2? _____

❺ Which columns have the same number of units? _____

❻ How many units are in column 8? _____

❼ How many more units are in column 6 than in column 5? _____

❽ How many fewer units are in column 3 than in column 7? _____

❾ If the number of ▲s doubled in column 2, how many units would be in the column? _____

❿ Which column has 1/3 of the units of column 6? _____

G __ __   __ __ __ __ __ __ __ __.
   6   2 10 5 1 4 7 3 8 9

Solar System

Name _____ Date _____

What is the smartest member of the solar system? _____

To find the answer, solve the problems on page 59. Then plot the ordered pairs and connect the points. The picture you make will help you solve the riddle.

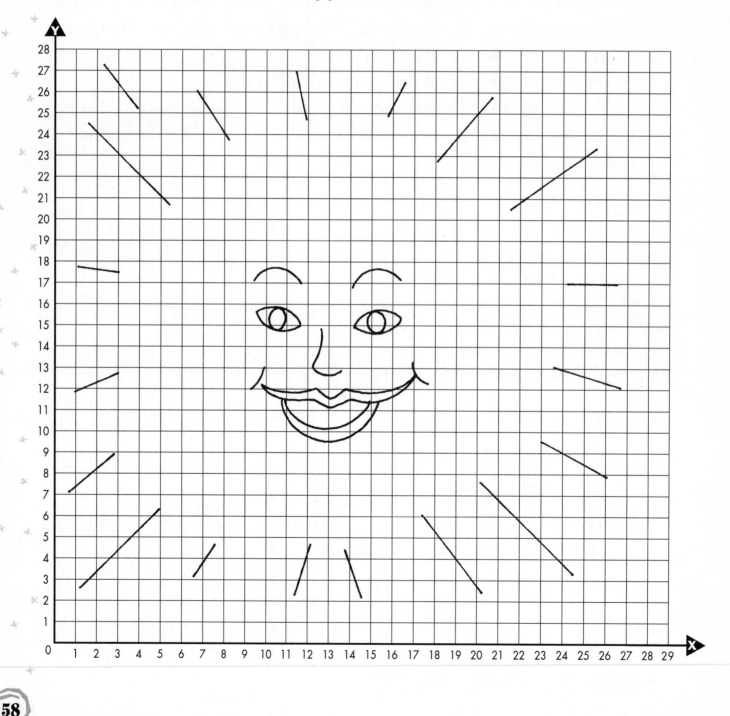

Solar System

Name _____ Date _____

1. Look at number 1, left. The number in the first column is the X coordinate in an ordered pair.
2. Look at the numbers in the second column. Write the missing number so that the fractions are equivalent. The missing number is the Y coordinate.
3. Write the X and Y coordinates in the third column to make an ordered pair. The first one has been done for you.
4. Determine the ordered pairs for the rest of the chart.
5. Plot the ordered pairs on the graph on page 58 in the order they are given. Then use a straightedge to connect the points in the order you plotted them. Can you solve the riddle?

	X Coordinate	Y Coordinate	Ordered Pair
1.	14	$\frac{4}{9} = \frac{12}{27}$	(14, 27)
2.	15	$\frac{3}{7} = \frac{9}{}$	
3.	17	$\frac{6}{9} = \frac{}{36}$	
4.	17	$\frac{2}{3} = \frac{}{30}$	
5.	22	$\frac{1}{2} = \frac{}{46}$	
6.	19	$\frac{2}{6} = \frac{6}{}$	
7.	25	$\frac{1}{3} = \frac{}{57}$	
8.	20	$\frac{1}{8} = \frac{2}{}$	
9.	26	$\frac{2}{9} = \frac{}{63}$	
10.	21	$\frac{1}{10} = \frac{}{130}$	
11.	25	$\frac{2}{5} = \frac{4}{}$	
12.	20	$\frac{1}{5} = \frac{}{55}$	
13.	25	$\frac{2}{11} = \frac{}{33}$	
14.	19	$\frac{2}{3} = \frac{6}{}$	
15.	20	$\frac{1}{5} = \frac{}{25}$	
16.	17	$\frac{1}{7} = \frac{}{49}$	
17.	17	$\frac{1}{44} = \frac{}{88}$	
18.	13	$\frac{2}{3} = \frac{4}{}$	

	X Coordinate	Y Coordinate	Ordered Pair
19.	9	$\frac{1}{7} = \frac{}{14}$	
20.	10	$\frac{1}{12} = \frac{}{84}$	
21.	7	$\frac{1}{19} = \frac{}{95}$	
22.	8	$\frac{1}{4} = \frac{2}{}$	
23.	3	$\frac{2}{2} = \frac{6}{}$	
24.	7	$\frac{1}{9} = \frac{}{99}$	
25.	3	$\frac{2}{5} = \frac{4}{}$	
26.	6	$\frac{1}{7} = \frac{}{91}$	
27.	1	$\frac{3}{7} = \frac{6}{}$	
28.	6	$\frac{3}{8} = \frac{6}{}$	
29.	3	$\frac{1}{5} = \frac{}{95}$	
30.	8	$\frac{2}{3} = \frac{12}{}$	
31.	5	$\frac{1}{7} = \frac{}{161}$	
32.	10	$\frac{9}{10} = \frac{18}{}$	
33.	10	$\frac{11}{12} = \frac{22}{}$	
34.	12	$\frac{2}{3} = \frac{14}{}$	
35.	14	$\frac{9}{15} = \frac{}{45}$	

Answer Key

Page 5
1. The high score is 93. The low score is 47.
2. The range is 46.
3. 47, 73, 81, 86, 93; median score is 81.
4. 76; **5.** 15
Super Challenge: Answers will vary.

Page 6

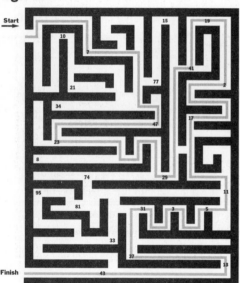

Page 7
1. 79; **2.** 3,649; **3.** 9,999; 999; **4.** 30,499; 20,499

Page 8
The ice cream thieves are wearing shirts with the numbers 11, 19, and 47.

Page 9
thousandths place: 12.103; 78.883; 88.913; 6.153; 0.193; 9.103; 0.113; 9.043; 8.193; 9.103; 0.013; 3.703
hundredths place: 6.13; 12.73; 0.13; 1.736; 12.832; 6.93; 8.03; 2.03; 9.13; 9.73; 0.03; 7.13
tenths place: 2.30; 1.36; 4.3; 8.37; 8.3; 8.37; 1.3; 0.3; 9.3; 8.34; 5.379.3

Page 10

Page 11

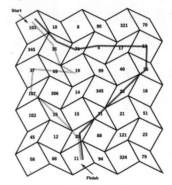

Page 12

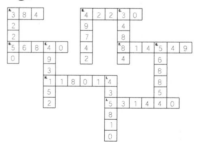

Darker line = "genius" path
Lighter line = "superstar" path

Page 13

Page 14
1. 22, 25; **2.** 14, 15; **3.** 29, 31
4. 44, 45, 46; **5.** 17, 19, 21; **6.** 13, 52

Page 15
1. 1,352; **2.** 3,278; **3.** 8,200; **4.** 2,346
5. 3,450; **6.** 9,610; **7.** 7,551; **8.** 3,139

	A	B	C	D
E	3	2	7	8
F	1	3	5	2
G	3	4	5	0
H	9	6	1	0

9. 9,318; **10.** 3,641; **11.** 7,495
12. 2,173; **13.** 5,631; **14.** 9,572
15. 1,397; **16.** 8,153

	A	B	C	D
E	9	3	1	8
F	5	6	3	1
G	7	4	9	5
H	2	1	7	3

Page 16
1. 35; **2.** 45; **3.** 56; **4.** 50; **5.** 60; **6.** 72

Page 17
1. 9:24 a.m.; **2.** 9:00 p.m.; **3.** 25; **4.** 61

Page 18

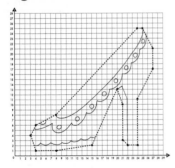

Page 19
1. 3.5, 2.5; **2.** 4.25, 4; **3.** 0.6, 0.4 **4.** 4.8, 5.8

Pages 20-21

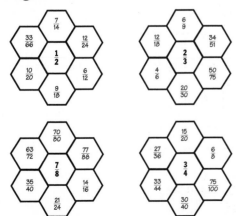

Answer: She was tired of working with heels.

Page 22

Page 23
1. 3/6, 6/12; **2.** 3/7
3. 3/12; 12/48; **4.** 9/15, 15/25
5. 8/12, 12/18; **6.** 2/4, 4/8; 4/8, 8/16

Page 24

Page 25
1. .25; **2.** .25; **3.** .23; **4.** .75
5. .06; **6.** .6; **7.** .22; **8.** .44
9. .88; **10.** .75; **11.** .67; **12.** .45
13. .75; **14.** 4.6; **15.** .63; **16.** .44
17. .88; **18.** .35; **19.** 1.13; **20.** 1.25

Page 26

9.09 < 9.18	18.3 > 18.03	31.8 > 30.4	54.1 > 54
0.8 < 0.82	29.5 > 28.5	3.57 > 3.55	8.31 > 8.30
6.71 < 6.75	41.05 < 41.5	0.009 < 0.09	5.20 > 5.10
1.09 > 1.08	9.33 < 9.36	21.45 < 21.5	3.22 > 3.12
7.91 > 7.90	0.102 < 0.12	0.73 > 0.71	93.4 > 93.0

Answer key

Page 27

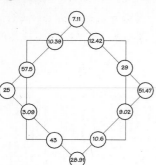

Page 28
1. 4.234; **2.** 12.584; **3.** 114.925; **4.** 203.460

Page 29
1. 109.6; **2.** 52.8; **3.** 450; **4.** 343.98
5. 504.72; **6.** 278.4; **7.** 456.75—PEANUTS
8. 11.75; **9.** 385.2; **10.** 91.6; **11.** 527.25—A CAR

Page 30
1. 168, 252, 336, 420, 504; **2.** 110, 165, 330, 550, 825
3. 100, 150, 200, 250, 300; **4.** $5.50, $8.25, $11.00, $13.75, $16.50
5. 175; 350; 525; 1,050; 2,100; **6.** $13.00, $19.50, $26.00, $39.00, $52.00
7. 84, 126, 210, 420, 630; **8.** 54¢, $1.44, $2.16, $2.52, $2.88
9. $8, $12, $16, $20, $24; **10.** 720; 1,440; 2,880; 5,760; 11, 520

Page 31
Order of answers within rows may vary:

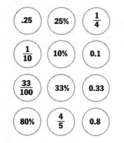

Page 32

87%	87.5	$\frac{7}{8}$	.875	87½%	.24	24%
$\frac{25}{100}$	$\frac{3}{5}$	50%	$\frac{12}{5}$	2.4	24.0%	$\frac{6}{20}$
0.25	.03	.50	$\frac{7}{25}$	$\frac{1}{5}$	.20	20%
25%	30%	$\frac{2}{4}$	.27	$\frac{6}{8}$	0.75	75%
$\frac{1}{8}$	0.125	12.5%	27%	.27	$\frac{10}{25}$	2.5
70%	$\frac{18}{40}$	.45	45%	$\frac{2}{4}$	.40	40%
0.7	$\frac{112}{200}$	1.12	112%	$\frac{11}{112}$	40%	.405
$\frac{4}{5}$	.0625	62.5%	62%	$\frac{7}{25}$	.28	28%

Page 33
1. The ratio was 1:3. **2.** The ratio was 1:2.
3. Sixteen cousins were girls. The ratio was 2:1.
4. The ratio was 1:3. **5.** The ratio was 4:3.
6. The ratio was 1:9. **7.** The ratio was 20:1.
8. Eighty ants were red. **9.** Fifty percent of the ants were late.
Wrap It Up! A total of 240 ants were not hungry.

Page 34
1. 24, 35, 48; **2.** 89, 121, 185; **3.** 8, 4, 2; **4.** 36, 25, 16
5. 79, 75, 71; **6.** 512, 2048, 8192; **7.** 42, 35, 27; **8.** 18, 15, 12
9. 36, 44, 52; **10.** 9, 11, 13; **11.** 19, 26, 34; **12.** 5/6, 6/7, 7/8
13. 18, 27, 38; **14.** 13, 21, 34; **15.** 20, 24, 28
16. 10/11, 12/13, 14/15; **17.** 243, 729, 2187; **18.** 16, 22, 29

Page 35
1. Answers will vary; if you add the sum of the digits, they equal nine.
2. All are evenly divisible by 3.
3. 2004, 2008, 2012, 2016, 2020, 2024, 2028, 2032, and 2034
4. 165; 1999; 802; **5.** Answers will vary.

Page 36
1. 3 n, 12 d; **2.** 8 d, 2 q
3. 15 n, 5 d, 15 q; **4.** $1.00, $1.50, $2.50

Page 37
	Hanlon's	Murray's		Hanlon's	Murray's
1.	$1.40	$ .92	**2.**	.31	.38
3.	.61	.83	**4.**	.55	.58
5.	.57	.44	**6.**	.40	.38
7.	.49	.31	**8.**	.37	.30

Page 38
1. 264 inches; **2.** 6 inches; **3.** 16 inches
4. Both mirrors have the same perimeter.
5. Mirror A has a bigger perimeter than Mirror B by 2 inches.
Super Challenge: The mirror's width is 22 inches, and its perimeter is 66 inches.

Page 39
A. 1F, 2G, 3B, 4C **or** A, 5E, 6I, 7E, 8H, 9G, 10G, 11C
B. 1B, 2F, 3D, 4I, 5F, 6E, 7A, 8D, 9I, 10F, 11I
C. 1H, 2C, 3C, 4G, 5G, 6C, 7F, 8I, 9B, 10C **or** A, 11F

Page 40

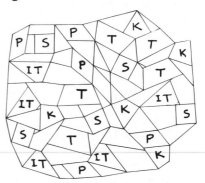

Page 41
1. 6, 12, 8, 1; **2.** 24, 8; **3.** 8, 2

Page 42
1. $540; **2.** $170.88; **3.** $49.50; **4.** $22.50
5. $276.48; **6.** $90.00; **7.** $246; **8.** $199.80

Page 43
1. railway signal; **2.** ironing board; **3.** gas mask
4. cash register; **5.** ear muffs; **6.** ballpoint pen
7. hearing aid; **8.** windshield wiper

Page 44
1. c; **2.** d; **3.** a; **4.** b; **5.** c; **6.** b; **7.** b; **8.** d

Page 45
1. 11 feet; **2.** 37.5 gallons; **3.** 15 cups; **4.** 24 hours
5. 6 gallons; **6.** 6549 weeks; **7.** 50 yards; **8.** 74 feet
9. 89 dozen; **10.** 198 pounds; **11.** 2,000 pounds; **12.** 230 feet

Page 46
1. M; **2.** R; **3.** S; **4.** I; **5.** E; **6.** A; **7.** E; **8.** I; **9.** M; **10.** Y
What do baby sweet potatoes sleep in?
Their "yammies"

Page 47

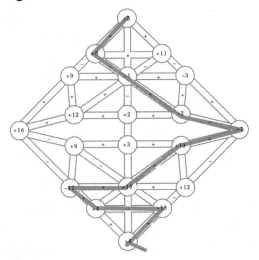

Page 48
1. 12, 4; **2.** 12; **3.** 34; **4.** 14, 4, 2; **5.** 12

Page 49
1. 4, 9; **2.** ±12, ±8; **3.** 9; **4.** 64, 4

Page 50

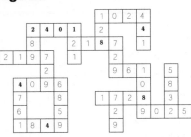

$7^4 = 2,401$; $3^7 = 2,187$; $43^2 = 1,849$; $95^2 = 9,025$; $33^2 = 1,089$

$27^2 = 729$; $21^2 = 441$; $11^2 = 121$; $17^2 = 289$; $2^7 = 128$
$18^3 = 5,832$; $12^3 = 1,728$; $8^4 = 4,096$; $4^5 = 1,024$; $3^6 = 729$
$13^3 = 2,197$; $3^6 = 729$; $31^2 = 961$; $19^3 = 6,859$; $69^2 = 4,761$

Page 51
1. 66; **2.** 95; **3.** 90; **4.** 93

Page 52
1. 6, 21; **2.** 12, 44; **3.** 51, 88; **4.** 24

Page 53
1. 2 blocks; **2.** 3 blocks; **3.** 7 blocks; **4.** 7 blocks; **5.** 4 blocks
Super Challenge: Riding up 3rd Street

Page 54
1. 5 pieces; **2.** 25 pieces; **3.** 10 pieces
4. 7 smashed pumpkins; **5.** 45 pieces
Super Challenge: 95 pieces

Page 55
Pizza Shop Choices: **1.** 55; **2.** 80; **3.** 55; **4.** 30; **5.** 20; **6.** 10
Video Store Rentals: **1.** 184; **2.** 126; **3.** 79; **4.** 37; **5.** 47; **6.** 16
7. 11; **8.** 26

Page 56
1. Rudy practiced the longest on Day 8.
2. Rudy practiced less than 5 minutes on Day 5.
3. Rudy practiced more than 45 minutes on Days 8, 9, and 11.
4. Rudy practiced between 10 and 20 minutes on Day 10.
5. Yes; **6.** Yes; **7.** Less; **8.** 25 minutes
Wrap It Up! Answers will vary.

Page 57
1. 5 units; **2.** column 7; **3.** column 3; **4.** 20 units
5. columns 1 and 5; **6.** 25 units; **7.** 15 units; **8.** 30 units
9. 40 units; **10.** column 4
How can you dive without getting wet? Go skydiving.

Pages 58-59

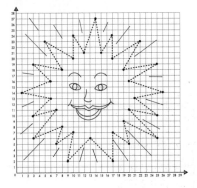

Answer: The sun is the brightest.

Instant Skills Index